Mastering AWS Config Rule Compliance Troubleshooting

Table of Contents

Chapter 1. Introduction

Special Report: "Mastering AWS Config Rule Compliance Troubleshooting"

Navigating the landscapes of cloud compliance can feel like traversing a maze shrouded in complex technical jargon. Precisely why we have compiled this Special Report titled "Mastering AWS Config Rule Compliance Troubleshooting" for you. We've peeled back the layers of this highly technical topic to provide you with clear, comprehensive guidance on managing AWS Config rules. Our objective is straightforward: to arm you with the tools and understanding needed to swiftly resolve any compliance issues that may arise within your AWS environment. This isn't about selling you a dream; instead, we offer you accessible knowledge, pragmatically preparing you for the realities of AWS Config management. Here's a promise: by the end of this report, the fog of confusion and apprehension surrounding AWS Config Rule Compliance will have cleared significantly for you. So, brace yourselves for an enlightening journey into the depths of AWS compliance troubleshooting. Let's demystify the intricate together!

Chapter 2. Introduction to AWS Config

AWS Config is a fully managed service that provides users with the resources to assess, audit, and evaluate the configurations of their AWS resources. AWS Config is essential because it allows users to continuously monitor and record their resource configurations and also enables to automate the evaluation of recorded configurations against desired configurations.

AWS Config simplifies compliance auditing, security analysis, change management, and operational troubleshooting. By turning on AWS Config, the system starts observing your resource configurations, their relationships to one another, and their changes over time.

2.1. Key Features of AWS Config

The AWS Config utilities include resource Discovery and Tracking, Compliance Monitoring, and Change Management.

2.1.1. Resource Discovery and Tracking

AWS Config has the capacity to discover existing AWS resources, construct a complete inventory, and then track changes to the configurations over time. This catalogue can be used to verify compliance with specific standards, measure your resource configurations against best practice guidelines, or analyse changes for troubleshooting purposes.

2.1.2. Compliance Monitoring

Utilising AWS Config's rules, the system can analyse changes to resources and evaluate whether these alterations are compliant with specific policies. More than just a resource inventory, AWS Config's rules offer a dynamic, continuously auditable, policy-as-code record of the configuration state of your landscape.

2.1.3. Change Management

By utilising AWS Config's ability to track changes over time, users can drive a robust process for managing change across their environment, reviewing and approving changes to configurations and more importantly, understanding the effects of changes on the overall environment.

2.2. Configuration and Compliance Data

A critical aspect of AWS Config is the continuous capture and analysis of resource configuration and compliance data.

2.2.1. Configuration Data

AWS Config records the state of your AWS resources and their associated relationships. Configuration items represent snapshots of a resource's attributes and connections at a specific point, and AWS Config records a configuration item whenever it detects a change to a resource.

These Configuration items can provide insight such as:

- What were the block device mappings of an Amazon EC2 instance at the time of launch?

- Was an Amazon RDS database instance publicly accessible at a specific point in the past?

- How frequently do network settings on a security group change?

2.2.2. Compliance Data

AWS Config rules allow AWS Config to continuously track the compliance status of AWS resources and AWS managed policies. Essentially, AWS Config rules rely on AWS Managed rules and Custom Rules.

AWS Managed Rules are predefined, customizable rules that AWS Config uses to evaluate whether your AWS resources comply with common best practices. On the other hand, Custom Rules let you define the code for the AWS Config Rule's desired behavior.

2.3. Working of AWS Config

AWS Config operates by recording configuration changes that occur among your resources and delivering an updated configuration snapshot on a periodic basis. You can also check compliance status against AWS Config rules.

2.3.1. AWS Config Recorder

The Config recorder is the entity that records the configuration changes that occur in your account and delivers the updated configuration snapshot.

2.3.2. AWS Config Rules

As mentioned, AWS Config utilizes managed and custom rules to assess your resource configurations. When you customize these rules to suit your requirements, and then turn these rules on, AWS Config evaluates your resources' configurations according to these rules.

2.4. AWS Config Versus Other AWS Services

There are other AWS services that, on first glance, might appear to offer similar capabilities to AWS Config, but they differ in several key aspects.

2.4.1. AWS Config Vs. AWS CloudTrail

While both services handle AWS governance, compliance, risk auditing, and operational auditing, they essentially deal with different kinds of data. AWS Config deals with configuration settings whereas AWS CloudTrail focuses on user activity.

2.4.2. AWS Config Vs. AWS Trusted Advisor

While AWS Config lets you define and monitor compliance of your own resource configurations, AWS Trusted Advisor draws upon best practices learned from serving hundreds of thousands of AWS customers to provide real-time guidance to help provision your resources following AWS best practices.

Through continuous monitoring, capturing of configuration histories, and availability of AWS Config rules for resources, AWS Config has proven to be a valuable resource in maintaining and enforcing compliance standards. By leveraging its key features, you will not only have greater visibility into your AWS resource configurations but also reinforce the security around them. Moreover, you can more effectively manage changes, strengthening your overall operational health.

Chapter 3. Understanding AWS Config Rules

Before we delve deeper into troubleshooting, it's crucial to understand the basics of AWS Config Rules.

AWS Config is a fully managed service that provides you with insights into the configurations of your AWS resources, consequently rendering comprehensive visibility into your AWS infrastructure. It continuously observes and records your AWS resource configurations, making it easier for you to assess, audit, and evaluate the configurations of your AWS resources.

3.1. What is AWS Config Rules?

With AWS Config, you get AWS Config Rules – a feature enabling you to automate the evaluation of recorded configurations against desired settings. This arrangement allows you to simplify compliance auditing, manage security, streamline operational best practices, and assess your overall operational health.

AWS Config Rules becomes savvy when you leverage AWS managed rules – predefined, customizable rules that AWS Config uses to evaluate whether your AWS resource configurations comply with common best practices. Herein lies the power of customization – you can write your own custom rules according to your unique compliance requirements using AWS Lambda.

3.2. AWS Config Rules Configuration

Now, to set up AWS Config Rules, you need to understand its two components: the AWS Lambda function and a trigger.

Lambda Function: AWS Lambda is an event-driven, serverless computing platform by AWS. A rule leverages AWS Lambda function to express the logic that evaluates whether your AWS resources comply with the rule.

Triggers: AWS Config Rules supports two types of triggers – period and configuration change. A rule can be triggered either by a configuration change to a resource or at a periodic frequency (currently, a rule can only trigger a frequency no more than once every 24 hours).

3.3. Working of AWS Config Rules

For a deeper understanding, let's step through how AWS Config Rules function in practice.

Whenever there's a configuration change or at a periodic frequency (whichever trigger you've set), AWS Config Rules invokes the related AWS Lambda function, passing the configuration details of the recorded AWS resources.

Within the Lambda function, your defined logic is executed to evaluate the configuration item against the desired configuration. Next, the Lambda Function returns the evaluation results to AWS Config.

These results are translated into compliance statuses – Compliant, Noncompliant, or Not applicable – and are then made available via AWS Config console, APIs, or through Amazon SNS notifications.

3.4. Implementing AWS Managed Rules

Setting up AWS Managed Rules is quite straightforward. You select the rules from the Config console, Config APIs, or SDKs based on the resources you want to evaluate. Each of these rules has input parameters that allow you to specify the details of the rule, thus tailoring it to suit your environment.

Once AWS Managed Rules are set up, AWS Config invokes them whenever there are configuration changes or at periodic intervals.

3.5. Custom Rules with AWS Lambda

To define a custom rule, you build an AWS Lambda function that encapsulates the evaluation logic. AWS provides the AWS Config Rule Development SDK to ease your AWS Lambda function creation process.

Post creation, you specify the AWS Lambda function ARN and choose the appropriate trigger type while defining your custom rule in AWS Config.

Remember, the AWS Config SDK does not include tests. Hence, it's recommended to use stub tests, a testing method where you simulate the behaviors of software components (also known as stubs).

In conclusion, mastering AWS Config Rules requires grasping how to mold them to your unique use cases. By understanding the functionality of AWS Config Rules, from the configuration to implementation, we set the stage for diving into AWS Config Rule Compliance Troubleshooting in the next chapter. Knowledge of how these rules play out in real-world scenarios equips you better for swift identification and resolution of any compliance challenges that may arise.

Chapter 4. Setting Up AWS Config

Setting up AWS Config, in essence, is creating the nervous system for your AWS environment. By establishing robust AWS Config rules, you can monitor changes across your resource types in real-time, helping you achieve adherence to industry-wide best practices and your own internal policies for AWS resources. Let's dive into the step-by-step process of setting up AWS Config and creating rules:

4.1. Preliminary Steps

Before you even start setting up AWS Config, certain prerequisites need to be met. To begin with, AWS Config requires appropriate permissions to deliver configuration items to an S3 bucket present in your account, and send notifications through Amazon SNS. The AWS management console happens to be the simplest way to set up AWS Config.

Here is a rundown of what needs to be ready before setting up AWS Config:

1. An AWS account

2. Access to the AWS Management Console

With these preconditions met, let's now dive into the step-by-step guide to setting up AWS Config.

4.2. Step 1: Create an S3 Bucket

The first step in setting up AWS Config is creating an Amazon S3 bucket, a scalable and secure destination for storing your configuration items. Configuration items, as you might know, are records of configurations for your AWS resources.

You can either create an S3 bucket from scratch or allow AWS Config to do it on your behalf. To create a bucket manually, follow these steps:

1. Login to the AWS S3 management console.

2. Click on 'Create bucket.'

3. Choose a name and region.

4. In 'Configure options,' select the defaults.

5. Set the permissions as per your requirements under 'Set permissions.'

6. Click 'Create bucket.'

4.3. Step 2: Set Up an Amazon SNS Topic

In the next step, an Amazon SNS topic is to be set up to which AWS Config can send configuration change notifications. The process involve:

1. Navigate to the Amazon SNS console and click on 'Topics.'

2. Click on 'Create topic.' You can either choose a 'Standard' or 'FIFO' type. For the purpose of AWS Config, 'Standard' would suffice.

3. Name the topic and note down the ARN (Amazon Resource Name) for further setup.

4. Click 'Create topic.'

Make sure your SNS topic is in the same region as your AWS Config and S3 bucket.

4.4. Step 3: Setting Up AWS Config

Now that you have the S3 bucket and the SNS topic set up, navigate to the AWS Config console to get started with the actual setup.

1. Click on 'Settings' on the dashboard.

2. Under 'Resource inventory,' tick 'Record all resources supported in this region' to keep records of all your AWS resources.

3. Under 'Delivery frequency,' choose the frequency at which the recorded changes are to be delivered to your S3 bucket.

Now, configure the Amazon S3 bucket where AWS Config will send and store your configuration changes:

1. Under 'Storage location,' select the S3 bucket that you've already created or let AWS Config create a new one for you.

2. Once you have selected your bucket, move on to the next field - Amazon SNS topic.

3. Here, enter the Amazon Resource Name (ARN) of the SNS topic that you've created earlier. Make sure to cross-verify the details

Many times, organizations choose to stream configuration changes, account auditing, or security incident responses to AWS Systems Manager, Amazon CloudWatch Logs, or AWS Lambda for real-time analysis and remediation. If you want AWS Config to deliver configuration changes to any of these Management Tools, tick the corresponding check box.

Following the steps above is a good start to your AWS Config journey. The process, of course, is more dynamic and varies according to the individual requirements of an organization. For finer control and specific compliance requirements, you can set up AWS Config Rules, which we'll explore in subsequent chapters.

This chapter was focused on the practical side of setting things up, but staying on top of AWS Config requires understanding of its underlying principles too, and a lot more. As we delve further into AWS Config, you'll learn to master various facets of this powerful tool. Let's continue on our journey to unravel these layers.

4.5. Wrapping Up

By this point, you have taken the initial steps towards establishing an AWS Config system for your business. Understanding these elementary steps is essential for managing your AWS resources effectively while meeting compliance requirements.

Up ahead, we will delve deeper, discussing more on AWS Config rules, how to create them, and how to handle noncompliance. As you navigate deeper, you'll grow more comfortable with AWS Config, becoming better equipped to troubleshoot issues and ensure compliance across your AWS resources. Let's proceed further into our exploration.

Chapter 5. Navigating Compliance Concepts

Cloud compliance might feel like an extraterrestrial concept when first encountered. Despite its complex overtones, this crucial facet of managing a cloud environment can be simplified when we break it down into digestible components, and AWS Config plays a vital role in achieving this undertaking. Delving into its depths, we can explore its layers and understand the interactions that lead to the 'compliance' or 'noncompliance' state.

5.1. Understanding the AWS Config Framework

At the heart of the AWS Config service is its ability to evaluate your AWS resources against desired configurations and provide visibility into your environment's compliance status. It does this through rules - essentially predefined or custom definitions that describe the ideal state of a resource. Non-compliance occurs when AWS Config finds a difference between the actual state of a resource and its acceptable configuration, as per these rules.

NOTE Remember, AWS Config doesn't change your resources. It simply monitors the AWS environment and notifies you of noncompliant resources.

5.2. Config Rules - Desired State Descriptions

There are different types of AWS Config rules, including AWS Managed rules and Customer Managed rules. AWS Managed rules are predefined, offering specific, ready-to-use configuration checks, while Customer Managed rules allow you to define your own configuration logic, typically via AWS Lambda.

The Config Rule compliance is the evaluation of these rules, which are periodically checked or triggered based on specific events in your environment. Thus, understanding and managing these rules is at the crux of exploring AWS Config.

5.3. Compliance States

The results of the AWS Config rules' evaluation manifest in the form of compliance states. Either compliant, meaning the resource matches the required configuration, or non-compliant, indicating a mismatch. A crucial aspect is understanding that the non-compliance state isn't necessarily an error; it could simply be an indication of divergence from the set rules.

5.4. AWS Config Dashboard

The AWS Config Dashboard is a powerful interface enabling the viewing and management of compliance statuses at a glance. Compliance status can be tracked per rule, per resource type, and even per resource; furthermore, the dashboard provides insights into the historical compliance trend, which is valuable for compliance auditing.

5.5. Evaluating Compliance - AWS Config Rule Evaluation Process

The Config rule evaluation process underpins the entire compliance framework. This process can be divided into steps:

1. AWS Config identifies a configuration change.

2. The change triggers an AWS Config rule evaluation.

3. The results are compared against the configurations defined in the rule.

4. If a mismatch is found, the resource is reported as noncompliant.

It's important to note here that different resources can trigger evaluations at different times, leading to a staggered snapshot of compliance evaluations.

5.6. Resolving Non-Compliance

Noncompliance can stem from various reasons - from simple misconfigurations to more complex deviations. Solving these implies not just identifying the source of non-compliance but also remediating it effectively. Remediation can involve manual intervention or more automated processes through AWS Config's Remediation actions feature.

5.7. Managing Compliance Data

The AWS Config Rule Compliance History contributes greatly to managing compliance data. This feature delivers an evidence trail of compliance and non-compliance over time, beneficial for audits and in-depth compliance investigations.

In conclusion, navigating compliance concepts in AWS Config involves understanding the Config rules framework, how these rules evaluate compliance, and how to interpret and remediate discovered non-compliance, enriched by data from the Config Rule Compliance History. Now that we've explored these key concepts, let's move ahead to understand their intricate workings. Knowledge is your true companion in the journey of cloud compliance.

Chapter 6. Identifying & Analyzing Non-Compliant Resources

Understanding non-compliant resources is a critical factor in managing AWS Config rules. Non-compliant resources are the ones violating the conditions set through AWS Config rules. Identifying these rogue elements and analyzing the reasons behind their non-compliance is the primary step towards establishing a robust, compliant AWS environment.

6.1. Mechanics of Non-Compliance

First, let's dig into the mechanics of non-compliance. AWS records the configuration changes in your resources continuously. AWS Config's rules compare the recorded changes against desired configurations and designate resources as compliant or non-compliant.

The status of non-compliance does not necessarily suggest security vulnerability or operational inefficiency. But it does hint that the resource is running counter to the predefined conventions. The source of non-compliance can be broad-ranging. For example, a change in the EC2 instance type or a security group inadvertent modification could trigger the non-compliance.

6.2. Recognizing Non-Compliant Resources

Seeking out non-compliant resources requires detailed investigations, increasing your overall operational visibility and control.

- Look into the AWS Config console; within the 'Rules' page, a 'Compliance' column gives a current snapshot of compliant and non-compliant resources. Clicking on the 'Non-compliant resources' takes you to a detailed page listing all non-compliant resources.

- AWS CLI (Command Line Interface) is another potent tool. You can use the command 'describe-compliance-by-resource' to get a list of non-compliant resources.

- AWS SDKs provide programmatic access to AWS Config functionalities, enabling automated compliance checks.

6.3. Digging Deeper - Identifying Root Cause

Identifying the non-compliance cause is the subsequent essential step. AWS Config' evaluation history offers a wealth of insights here.

- AWS Config records the evaluations for each configuration item. The 'Evaluation Result' tab in the AWS Config console provides useful details about each evaluation like the rule, evaluated resource, compliance type, and timing.

- Delving into the 'Evaluation Result' of non-compliant resources helps pinpoint the exact reason and time for non-compliance.

- For a more in-depth look, AWS Config provides you an 'Evaluation timeline', enabling you to trace the alteration that led the resource to defy the rules.

6.4. Analyzing Evaluation Results - A Paradigm

Analyzing evaluation results demands a systematized approach.

1. Prioritize Concerns: Start by categorizing rules based on the impact they bear on the operations and security of your AWS environment. High-impact rules demand immediate attention.

2. Track Changes: Utilize Timeline view to trace the configuration change leading to non-compliance.

3. Investigate Resources: Analyze each non-compliant resource, starting from high-impact ones, to search for an overriding pattern or chronic issue. It helps to strategize future preventive measures.

4. Document Lessons: Keep a record of your discoveries, troubleshooting strategies, and resolutions. This documentation serves as an historical reference and contributes to a troubleshooting repository for future recurrence.

6.5. Dealing With False Positives

Occasionally, false positives - an item identified wrongly as non-compliant - can crop up due to errors in rule configuration. Here, fine-tuning the Config rules or employing AWS Config rule parameters can remedy the situation.

6.6. Automating Compliance Checks

To smooth the process of identifying non-compliant resources, you can automate compliance checks. AWS Systems Manager's 'Compliance Dashboard' simplifies and automates the compliance-checking process. The dashboard provides real-time insights into your system's compliance status, reduces necessary manual checks, and increases overall operational efficiency.

Identifying and analyzing non-compliant resources forms the foundation of your compliance troubleshooting strategy. By mastering these tasks, you can ensure your AWS environment remains robust and aligned with your business objectives. Though this journey may seem intricate, remember: the more you understand non-compliance, the more compliant your operations become.

Chapter 7. Common Troubleshooting Techniques in AWS Config

Managing and troubleshooting AWS Config Rules requires an effective approach that integrates a comprehensive understanding of the service's functionality, the types of challenges that may arise, and effective solutions toward resolving these issues.

7.1. Understanding AWS Config Rules and Evaluating Noncompliance

Before plunging into troubleshooting techniques, a solid grasp of AWS Config rules, non-compliance issues, and how they are evaluated is indispensable. AWS Config provides a detailed view of the configurations of AWS resources and evaluates these configurations against desired configurations expressed in the form of rules.

When AWS Config evaluates your resources, it compares them with the conditions present in your rules. If the resources deviate from these conditions, they are marked as non-compliant. Understanding this mechanism can help you identify potential non-compliance issues better while cutting down on the time needed for troubleshooting.

Some common rule evaluation errors include:

- 'Insufficient permissions to call other AWS services'

- 'Cannot invoke Lambda function'

- 'Size of configuration item changes is too large'

- 'Cannot execute Config rule because it is currently being deleted'

7.2. Troubleshooting 'Insufficient permissions'

If AWS Config Rule returns 'Insufficient permissions to call other AWS services', you may have made a permissions error. The Config service role might not have the necessary permissions to invoke actions on other AWS resources.

To resolve this, review the permissions of the AWS Config service role in IAM. Make sure it includes the 'config:*' actions and the necessary permissions for other AWS services it needs to interact with.

7.3. Addressing 'Cannot invoke lambda function' Error

This error typically arises when the AWS Config service cannot invoke the AWS Lambda function associated with a Config Rule. All Amazon-managed Config rules work by invoking a specific AWS Lambda function.

If you encounter this error, it could be because of the following reasons:

- The Lambda function doesn't exist or the ARN is incorrect.

- AWS Config service does not have permissions to execute the Lambda function.

- The Config rule is in a region different from the Lambda function.

Verify that the function in question exists and is in the same region as the AWS Config rule. Cross-check the ARN for any discrepancies.

Make sure that the IAM role associated with AWS Config has the 'lambda:InvokeFunction' permission.

7.4. Resolving 'Size of configuration item changes is too large'

This problem generally occurs when the size of a configuration item change exceeds the maximum limit, making it impossible for AWS Config to deliver the configuration item. Configuration items delivered by AWS Config are limited to a maximum size of 64 KB.

When this error occurs, consider splitting up your resources if possible, or reduce the number of changes that are happening simultaneously.

7.5. Dealing with 'Config rule is being deleted' Error

This issue crops up when you try to execute AWS Config while it's under deletion. The solution is simply to wait until the deletion process completes before trying to execute the Config rule again. Patience is key here.

7.6. Advanced Troubleshooting Techniques

Beyond these common errors, AWS Config Rule Compliance is susceptible to a wide range of issues that might require advanced troubleshooting.

For instance, when AWS Config Service cannot access S3 bucket to store configuration snapshots and compliance details, the cause could be:

- The Config service role doesn't have necessary permissions.

- The S3 bucket policy is not allowing Config service to deliver configuration snapshots.

To resolve such issues, validate that the necessary permissions are available and modify the S3 bucket policy to allow Config Service to deliver configuration items.

These comprehensive troubleshooting processes aren't an exhaustive representation of all the potential issues that can arise when working with AWS Config. They serve as a roadmap, guiding you through common problems and their sought-after solutions. With patience, practice, and thorough understanding, achieving efficient rule compliance troubleshooting goes from being a daunting task to a routine process. AWS Config is a dynamic service with its own nuances; understanding these is pivotal for seamless operations in an AWS environment and the effective resolution of compliance-related issues.

Chapter 8. Case Studies: Real-World AWS Config Troubleshooting Scenarios

Cloud compliance is not something one masters overnight. Hence, the importance of analyzing practical cases cannot be underestimated. Let's delve into some real-world AWS Config troubleshooting scenarios together.

8.1. The Disappearing Compliance Reports

Recently, a manufacturing company was faced with a mystery. Their pre-set AWS Config rules were supposed to send them compliance reports daily. However, these reports began to vanish abruptly. The IT team tasked with troubleshooting the problem was puzzled as the rules hitherto functioned without a glitch.

Nonetheless, they kicked off by verifying the AWS Config rules' status. They found the rules were COMPLIANT, yet no reports were coming through. Diving deeper, they discovered that the SNS topic associated with their AWS Config – where the compliance reports were supposed to land – was inadvertently deleted.

Here's how the issue was resolved, offering us valuable lessons:

1. They first created a new SNS topic and then edited the AWS Config settings to direct the compliance reports to this newly-created SNS topic.

2. They then confirmed the email subscription to ensure that the reports reach the relevant team members.

The lesson here is to ensure that all components, even those not directly managed by AWS Config, are preserved. It underlines the often-understated importance of having a solid backup strategy.

8.2. The Case of Non-compliance Status despite Fixing Resource Configurations

A financial services firm had consistent non-compliance status issues. A particular S3 bucket kept cropping up on their AWS Config Non-compliant resource list, despite them following all indications on how to fix the concerned resource's configuration.

To understand the problem, the team examined the AWS Config rule associated with this S3 bucket. They discovered the rule was set to check for public read permissions and stop if found as NON_COMPLIANT. However, they learnt that the bucket was used to host publicly accessible data, hence must have public read permissions.

The resolution path they decided to follow included:

1. They created a new rule to allow certain S3 buckets to be flagged as COMPLIANT even when public read permissions were accessible.

2. They then restricted public read permissions to only the necessary objects in the bucket, ensuring more secure access.

This case served to highlight the utility of custom rules in AWS Config and caution against restricting access too strictly, which can sometimes result in self-inflicted problems.

8.3. Misconfigured AWS Config Rule Failing to Track Resource Changes

An e-commerce firm noticed changes to some EC2 instances that weren't being reported by AWS Config. Suspecting the rules were misconfigured, the IT department got to work on troubleshooting.

Investigating the rule syntax, they observed that the IAM policy lacked the right permissions to track And report changes to EC2 instances. By further digging the issue, they learned the need for including "ec2:Describe*" and "ec2:List*" permissions to fully track changes.

To solve this, the team had to:

1. Modify the IAM policy attached to AWS Config rules to include necessary permissions for tracking and reporting changes.
2. Validate the changes by deliberately altering an EC2 instance's configuration and verifying if it was recorded.

Solving this issue reiterated the significance of configuring rules appropriately in AWS Config and being aware of the necessary permissions required.

8.4. Intermittently Failing AWS Config Rule

An online education platform was faced with a peculiar AWS Config issue - a rule would run and often show `COMPLIANT`, then sporadically report `NON_COMPLIANT` without any notable changes to the tracked resources.

Upon investigating, the team came across an unexpected cause. The rule was 'timing out' because it was running a scan on too many resources at once. This showed that even resource constraints could impact AWS Config performance.

The team used the following approach to resolve the issue:

1. They divided the resources into smaller groups to reduce the strain on the rules, thus preventing timeouts.

2. They then validated the solution by observing the rule status over a certain period.

This case study accentuated that resource allocation should always be taken into account in AWS Config rules.

Studying these scenarios helps in understanding how AWS Config rules operate in real-world situations, making you better equipped to troubleshoot arising issues in your own AWS environment. Remember, the goal is not the eradication of problems, but the ability to quickly identify and address challenges as they surface.

Chapter 9. Advanced Troubleshooting Techniques

Achieving proper compliance is a result of numerous gears working harmonically, and sometimes a single misaligned piece can derail the entire system. The intent of this section is to explore advanced troubleshooting techniques, once you've exhausted the basic AWS troubleshooting guides and still can't address the compliance hurdles.

9.1. Utilizing AWS Config Console

The AWS Config Console serves as the first line of response in times of compliance trouble. Here are some advanced steps to use this tool more effectively.

1. Validate Rule is associated with AWS Config: Navigate to the Config Console and select 'Rules' from the dashboard. If the rule in question is not listed, it's not associated with AWS Config.

2. Check for errors: If the rule status is not 'Deployed', the Config rule failed to create. Inspect the rule to spot any error messages.

3. Last AWS Config Rule run: If the rule status is 'Deployed', click on the rule and check the Last AWS Config rule run section. A failure in the last run indicates prevailing issues with AWS Config Rule execution.

9.2. Building Custom AWS Config Rules

Custom Config rules are powerful tools that help meet business-specific compliance needs. The troubleshooting process of custom rules involves validating the Lambda function, Config rule settings and S3 bucket.

1. Validate your Lambda Function: Use CloudWatch logs to check if the function is executing as expected. If you find errors, amend the function and redeploy the rule.

2. Determine if AWS Config is correctly triggering your Lambda function: Navigate to AWS Config console → Rules and see the rule frequency. If it's set to 'Periodic', ensure that AWS Config is correctly triggering the Lambda function.

3. Verify that your AWS Config Rule settings are correct: Ensure that the assigned resources are indeed what the custom rule should be checking. Also, verify that your trigger type aligns with your requirements.

4. Confirm S3 bucket permissions: AWS Config stores data in an S3 bucket. Ensure it has proper permissions to store data.

9.3. Analyzing and Correcting 'Non-Compliant' Rule

Sometimes, a rule may consistently flag resources as 'Non-Compliant', pushing you to investigate further.

1. Navigate to Config Dashboard → Rule details → Non-compliant resources. Note the accountId, ResourceId, and ResourceType.

2. Investigate the resource configuration using AWS CLI or SDKs, depending on its type.

3. Compare the resource configuration against the rule parameters.

4. Make the necessary changes and re-deploy the AWS Config Rule.

Application of these advanced troubleshooting procedures rectifies most AWS Config compliance issues. However, in instances where these steps still fall short, consider contacting AWS Support. They delve deeper into your setup and help resolve the problem more efficiently.

=== Leveraging AWS Config API

The AWS Config API provides a wealth of information, and its effective usage ensures more robust compliance troubleshooting.

1. Involve ListDiscoveredResources: To confirm if AWS Config is recording the desired resources, use the 'ListDiscoveredResources' action. If the intended resources are missing, verify AWS Config settings.

2. Review ConfigSnapshot: You can use the 'DeliverConfigSnapshot' action to generate and fetch a snapshot of your resource configurations.

9.4. Intertwining AWS CloudTrail with Config Rule Troubleshooting

AWS CloudTrail logs serve as a fantastic resource for AWS Config Rule troubleshooting.

1. Use the CloudTrail event history: Here, look for the 'PutEvaluations' entries corresponding to your Lambda function. Validate the input and output details.

2. Analyze CloudTrail logs: For deeper debugging, you can enable CloudTrail logs for your AWS Config and then dive into these logs for granular insights about the Config Rule execution flow.

9.5. Utilizing Trusted Advisor

Lastly, familiarize yourself with AWS Trusted Advisor – a real-time guide that inspects your environment and suggests improvements based on AWS defined best practices. It's especially helpful when troubleshooting a complex AWS Config compliance setup.

Remember, mastering AWS Config Rule Compliance Troubleshooting is about being proactive. Constantly analyze, validate, and tweak your environments based on the rich insights that these tools provide. The path to achieving and maintaining compliance need not be a convoluted affair. With these advanced tactics at your disposal, you possess the ability to conquer the most challenging compliance scenarios.

Chapter 10. Maintaining Ongoing Compliance in AWS

Compliance in the AWS environment is an ongoing task requiring constant vigilance, updating, and auditing. Maintaining compliance involves understanding AWS Config rules, monitoring changes, interpreting results, and performing remediation tasks to ensure security and compliance of the AWS resources to organizational policies.

10.1. Understanding AWS Config Rules

AWS Config Rules are the fundamental tools for compliance. They are AWS managed, customizable rules that assess the compliance of your AWS resources to the desired configurations. By defining appropriate Config rules, you can ensure that your resources comply with specific standards, conventions, and regulations. Understanding these rules is not just about knowing what they are, but also understanding how they work and how to effectively use them.

AWS Config rules can be categorized into two types: AWS managed rules and custom rules. AWS managed rules are predefined rules provided by AWS. These rules cover common compliance requirements and can conveniently be set up. Custom rules, on the other hand, offer flexibility for your unique compliance requirements. They are user-defined and involve writing AWS Lambda functions to specify desired configurations.

10.2. Continuous Monitoring and Recording

Continuous monitoring is essential in maintaining ongoing compliance. AWS Config records the configuration states of AWS resources and captures detailed resource configuration histories. It monitors changes and logs alterations in between. This is particularly important because it allows you to revert to a previous configuration if unforeseen complications arise due to changes.

Keeping track of changes enables easy auditing and provides a stream of evidence for compliance requirements. By default, AWS Config records all resources, but you can also choose to record a subset of resources.

10.3. Interpreting AWS Config Rules Compliance Results

Interpretation is as important as monitoring. AWS Config displays compliance results that allow you to understand whether your resources are in compliance or not. The AWS Management console provides a compliance dashboard, which displays an overview of your compliance status.

Each Config rule reports compliance as either `COMPLIANT`, indicating the resource is in compliance with the rule, or `NON_COMPLIANT`, showing a breach of the compliance rule. Additionally, for `NON_COMPLIANT` resources, AWS Config provides an accompanying explanation detailing the nature of the deviation.

10.4. Compliance Remediation

Once a `NON_COMPLIANT` result is recorded, remediation steps have to be initiated. AWS Config supports automated remediation by letting you associate remediation actions with Config rules. If a resource is found non-compliant against a particular rule, AWS Config executes the assigned remediation action.

To effectively employ remediation actions, it's essential to understand the various remediation controls offered by AWS. AWS offers built-in remediations that cover common tasks such as modifying security group rules, patching EC2 instances, and updating S3 bucket policies.

But what if AWS doesn't provide a built-in remediation action for your situation? That's where custom remediation comes in. AWS allows you to create your own remediation actions using AWS Systems Manager Automation documents. To use custom remediation, you specify an AWS Systems Manager Automation document (SSM document), and AWS Config executes it when non-compliance is detected.

10.5. Compliance Reporting

Compliances are not just about maintaining them; it's also about demonstrating that you have upheld them. AWS Config offers several methods to report on your compliance status. You could do this through the AWS Management console, AWS CLI, or AWS Config API.

AWS Config aggregates compliance results per rule, per resource, and overall account compliance. This report is useful for a quick overview of your compliance status. For a more detailed analysis, you can make use of AWS Config's compliance timeline feature which provides compliance history of your resources.

In addition, AWS Config can deliver configuration snapshots and configuration history files to an S3 bucket of your choice. These files provide detailed views of resource configurations and changes, helpful for in-depth audits.

Maintaining ongoing compliance in AWS requires aligning your resources with AWS Config rules, continuously monitoring and recording changes, accurately interpreting compliance results, efficiently performing remediation tasks, and effectively reporting compliance status. By mastering these elements, you can ensure the safety, security, and compliance of your resources in the AWS environment.

Chapter 11. Final Thoughts: Building a Resilient AWS Compliance System

As we round off our comprehensive voyage through the realm of AWS Config rule compliance troubleshooting, it's important to concretize our newfound understanding by strategically shaping a resilient AWS compliance system. This chapter serves as a sum-up of our expedition so far, providing critical action points that underpin the creation of a robust and durable system.

11.1. Understanding the Core Principles

To build a resilient AWS compliance system, it's imperative to understand the core principles that guide its operation. AWS Config rules serve as guardrails to monitor configuration changes against the conditions set by the rules. Remember, a resilient system reduces the occurrence of noncompliant resources and also enables rapid troubleshooting when issues arise.

Resiliency in this context means creating a system that is effective, flexible, reliable, and manageable. We achieve these attributes by focusing on automation, continuous monitoring, and regular assessment against well-defined objectives.

11.2. Establish Clear Compliance Objectives

A good start to building a resilient system begins with establishing clear compliance objectives. These objectives should align with your organization's overall goals and risk posture. Every rule you set up within your AWS Config should be purposeful and provide tangible value to your compliance operations.

Moreover, compliance objectives should not be set in stone. As regulatory and business environments evolve, so should your compliance objectives. Regular reviews ensure that your compliance system remains aligned with broader organizational objectives and continues to provide value.

11.3. Automate Compliance Processes

Automation is the heart of a strong compliance system in AWS. Automated processes not only reduce the human errors but also improve efficiency dramatically. AWS Config rules, once set up, work automatically to assess configuration changes and ensure compliance with defined regulations. Additionally, automated notifications about configuration changes aid in timely troubleshooting.

You can further enhance the automation by integrating AWS Config with other AWS services. For instance, Lambda functions can be set up to auto-remediate certain noncompliant resources, thereby reducing the manual effort needed to maintain compliance.

11.4. Continual Monitoring and Assessment

Continuous monitoring forms another essential pillar of a resilient AWS compliance system. AWS Config constantly monitors configurations, offering real-time visibility into your AWS resources, their relationships, and configuration history.

This constant observation allows you to detect noncompliant

resources and remediate them quickly. Remember, resiliency is not just about preventing noncompliance, but also about how swiftly and effectively you can correct it when it occurs.

11.5. Regular Updating and Education

AWS, like any major cloud provider, regularly updates and makes enhancements to its services. Thus, keeping yourself updated with the latest changes is necessary. Participating in regular training and subscribing to AWS update alerts help you effectively leverage new offerings and improve compliance operations.

Similarly, educating all relevant team members about AWS Config rules and their importance enhances overall compliance efficiency. This shared understanding and collaboration significantly contribute to the resilience of your AWS compliance system.

11.6. Conduct Regular Reviews and Audits

Lastly, the resilience of your compliance system can be strengthened by conducting regular reviews and audits of AWS Config rules. This not only validates the effectiveness of the rules but also helps identify any gaps in your compliance processes. Such proactive behavior bolsters your organisation's readiness for real-world audits and strengthens the overall compliance posture.

Building a resilient AWS compliance system is a continuous process requiring consistent efforts. By anchoring your system on the pillars of clear objectives, automation, continuous monitoring, regular updates, consistent education, and regular audits, you will forge an AWS compliance system that not only endures regulatory pressures but also enhances your organization's security, governance, and risk management strategies. Even though we have reached the end of this report, this marks just the beginning of your journey to mastering AWS Config Rule Compliance troubleshooting and management. Forge ahead! Keep learning, keep updating!